My first look at

A Butterfly

© Macmillan Publishers Ltd 1989

All rights reserved. No reproduction, copy or transmission of
this publication may be made without written permission.

No paragraph of this publication may be reproduced, copied or
transmitted save with written permission or in accordance with
the provisions of the Copyright Act 1956 (as amended), or under
the terms of any licence permitting limited copying issued by the
Copyright Licensing Agency, 334 Alfred Place, London WC1E 7DP.

Any person who does any unauthorised act in relation to this
publication may be liable to criminal prosecution and civil claims
for damages.

Published by
Macmillan Children's Books
A division of
MACMILLAN PUBLISHERS LTD
Houndmills, Basingstoke, Hampshire, RG21 2XS
and London
Companies and representatives
throughout the world.

© First edition: De Ruiter, Gorinchem, The Netherlands

Printed in Italy.

British Library Cataloguing in Publication Data

Andel, Lydia van
My first look at a butterfly
1. Butterflies
I. Title II. Sijl, Ineke van III. Agerbeek
Cherouke Ronkes IV Series
595. 78'9

ISBN 0-333-51758-X

Photographic Credits:

Jongman Naturfotografie

My first look at
A Butterfly

M

MACMILLAN

Look at the butterflies.
How many can you see?
They fly from flower to flower
looking for nectar.

Nectar is a kind of juice.
It is sweet.
Butterflies get nectar from flowers.
Where do butterflies come from?
Let's find out.

Look under the leaf.

Can you see the eggs?

They are very small.

There are lots of them.

Do you know what hatches out of them?

Look at these caterpillars.

There are lots of them.

Caterpillars hatch from eggs.

Can you see their little hairs?

And the spots on their backs?

Some caterpillars are smooth.

They don't have hairs.

Some caterpillars are green and some are yellow.

Caterpillars are greedy.
They eat and eat.
They eat all the leaves of a plant.
The caterpillars grow big and fat but
the plant is bare!

Where are the caterpillars?
They have disappeared.
What can you see on the plant?
A pupa... and another one.
Can you see them on the plant?
They look like brown leaves.
There are four of them.

Each caterpillar has turned into a pupa.
The pupa hangs from the plant.
It doesn't move at all.
It stays very still.

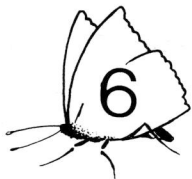

You can take the branch with the pupa on it.
If you put the branch into
a glass jar you can watch the pupa.
Put the jar where you can see the pupa.
What will happen next?

What is coming out of the pupa?
Is it a caterpillar?
No, it's a butterfly.

At first its wings are wet and soft.
So the butterfly stays very still.
Its wings will soon dry out in the sun.

The butterfly is ready to fly away.

It's wings are dry.

Isn't it beautiful.

Soon it will fly from flower to flower.

It will look for nectar.

You can watch it fly away.

Then you can look for more butterfly eggs.

Did you like this book?
There are lots more books for
you to read.

These are all the books in the
My first look at series:

 Spring

 Summer

 Autumn

 Winter

 Mushrooms

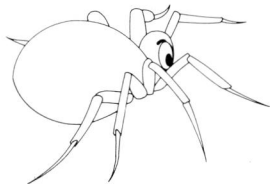 Spiders

 A Butterfly

 Honeybees